CW00395207

Book 1 of the Decency Journey series

HEALTHY LEADERSHIP

Anna Eliatamby

ISBN: 978-1-80443-007-1

British Library Cataloguing in Publication Data.
A catalogue record for this book is available from the British Library.

This pocketbook also contains some concepts from
the 2022 book, *Healthy Leadership and Organisations:
Beyond the Shadow Side*. Anna Eliatamby, Editor.

PREFACE

This pocketbook is part of a series on healthy leadership and organisations for decency. The aim is to encourage you to look at what is golden and shadow in your work as leaders and as organisations, so people can detox and heal. When we focus on the golden, and address the shadow, we are more likely to be decent in all we say and do.

Decency is 'honest, polite behaviour that follows accepted moral standards and shows respect for others' (Oxford Learners Dictionary).

We all contribute to what is golden (positive) and shadow (negative) in work and life. Mostly we operate from the golden side, but sometimes we function from the shadow side, and this holds us back as individuals and as organisations. We are all human and fallible.

Let's give ourselves permission to explore the positive and negative so that we create a better balance between the golden and shadow for ourselves and the wider world community. This way, we can contribute to a healthier world both for us now and for the generations to come. And we may yet achieve better decency for us all.

The titles in the Decency Journey Series are:

Healthy Leadership
Healthy Organisations
Coping In A Toxic Environment
Your Own Toxic Work Behaviours
Building an Organisational Mental Health and Well-being Strategy
Volcanoes, Personal Healing and Change
Our Journey for Diversity and Inclusion in Business

CONTENTS

OUR APPROACH

This pocketbook is based on a model that we describe in our book, *Healthy Leadership and Organisations: Beyond the Shadow Side.* Here are the key elements which we use as a basis for this pocketbook.

Healthiness is an essential ingredient for decency. Without it, we are likely to be unsuccessful.

WHAT IS OVERALL HEALTHINESS?

The words 'healthy' and 'healthiness' refer to physical health and, sometimes, mental health and well-being. These facets are important components for overall healthiness, and we suggest that there are others. These include synergy between purpose, values, and how we live and work; the impact of material resources and the environment, being willing to be open and listen to the incoming future, and how we live and cope with the shadow side.

All these factors, for overall healthiness, need to be coordinated with compassion and respect by our individual or organisational sense of Self. Collective responsibility for promoting the positive and addressing the negative should be present.

The golden refers to positive traits, whether individual or organisational, such as kindness, integrity, compassion, and working with purpose. The shadow includes dishonesty, bullying, and harassment.

WHAT IS HEALTHY LEADERSHIP?

Leadership is an individual and collective function that has many intentions. This usually includes an aim to serve human beings and/or something else. Some people operationalize leadership ethically and positively to serve others. Others will have another focus, such as a profit motive, alongside wanting to be ethical.

Healthy leadership happens when the individual or the group do their utmost to serve others ethically and respectfully, while acknowledging that there can be negativity and being willing to address it and heal. They remain flexible and open to sensing the incoming future.

Being and growing as a healthy leader ensures decency in yourself and in how you act at work.

WHAT IS A HEALTHY ORGANISATION?

Why do organisations exist? To enact a greater purpose, sometimes forgotten as the organisation becomes bigger and veers from the intended path.

A healthy organisation ensures it remains true to its purpose, and does no harm to humans or the planet. <u>Do no harm</u>. The organisation always endeavours to provide a nourishing culture and structure within which people can grow and flourish in their work to achieve that purpose. A healthy organisation works to recognise and address unhealthy elements, is amenable to change, and will consider possible futures while operating in the present.

Decency is seen as a core essential and its use flows naturally throughout the organization. People do not have to think about the need to be decent, they just are. Thus, the organization contributes to the greater decency we need for the world.

INTRODUCTION

Decency is a basic requirement.
We want and need decency.
We deserve decency in leadership and in our work.

What is decency in leadership? It requires us to be moral, ethical, and responsible. To be mindful, caring, and kind to others. Being decent means that we need to use our 'golden', positive leadership qualities, and be watchful of the negative, or 'shadow', ones we possess.

We all have golden and shadow sides to our leadership and personalities. We know our golden qualities and may or may not pay attention to the shadow side, which emerges at some point. Mine appears when I am tired; I become less patient and can be arrogant. Usually, I realise it and try to apologise and rectify the situation.

Most of us stay on the golden and positive side and rarely stray into the shadow side. A few of us prefer to operate from the shadow and negative side.

Regardless of which side they operate from, people rarely stop and think about how the shadow side can interfere in their leadership, and how it can lead to an imbalance in themselves and those they lead. For example, a dominant and domineering leader negatively affects the motivation and performance of their staff, even if the staff have control over their jobs.

If we are to make a true difference, then we need to give ourselves permission to explore the golden and shadow aspects of ourselves. In this way, we will become more decent and honourable in how we behave toward each other. We also need to investigate how we influence people in our work life and the wider organisation and community, and how they influence us. All these affect the extent to which we are golden or shadow as leaders.

Isn't it time to acknowledge our imperfections and develop a better balance between golden and shadow? Let's start the exploration.

ARE YOU READY?

As you begin this journey, please ensure you are ready for this and that it is the right time for you.

Embarking on a period of reflection can be challenging. It is important to choose a time that is right for you. Please stop and wait if it is not the right time for you to feel strong and supported as you ask yourself some tough questions. Reflect on the conditions that will help you get ready. Who could be your supporter? What could you do while you wait to help yourself become ready?

RAWINDA wanted to become more decent and honourable as a leader, but she was going through a divorce and had a new manager who was not very keen on supporting her. Rawinda wanted to expand her skills but waited until she was more settled. She wrote a list of her positives and kept them on her phone as a note. That was enough to sustain her for six months. She then explored her qualities as a leader by going on a course, with the reluctant permission of her manager.

A PLACE AND TIME FOR LEARNING

Remember to create time and space for yourself so that you can benefit from what you learn. Where do you want to be? When is the most relaxing time for you? What items do you want around you? How will you record your reflections?

You could allocate a day to do this or break it up into a series of one-hour slots. If you choose the latter, then please make sure that you stick to a schedule.

AMADOU set aside an hour for himself every weekend to explore his sense of Self. He negotiated a suitable time with his partner. William agreed he would leave the apartment for that hour so that Amadou could concentrate. William and Amadou prepared the study with snacks, and they bought a box in which Amadou could keep his exercises and reflections.

KEY ELEMENTS

WHAT IS HEALTHY LEADERSHIP?

Leadership is an individual and collective function that has many intentions. This usually includes an aim to serve human beings and/or something else. Some people operationalize leadership ethically and positively to serve others. Others will have another focus, such as a profit motive, alongside wanting to be ethical.

Healthy leadership happens when the individual or the group do their utmost to serve others ethically and respectfully, while acknowledging that there can be negativity and being willing to address it and heal. They remain flexible and open to sensing the incoming future.

Being and growing as a healthy leader ensures decency in yourself and in how you act at work.

PRESENCE AND USE OF GOLDEN AND SHADOW BEHAVIOURS

The concept of golden (positive) and shadow (negative) parts of us has its roots in ancient philosophies and traditions, including Buddhism. Carl Jung and Robert Johnson then used these ideas in their work. The golden and positive parts include kindness, compassion, honesty, and integrity in our behaviours, emotions, and thoughts. We know these aspects of ourselves, or at least assume that we do. Leadership programmes feature these, and we speak about them.

There is a range of shadow behaviors, thoughts, emotions, and actions. Some are harmless and benign, e.g., feeling too lazy to get up in time for work. Others may hinder us, such as being arrogant and withholding information from your team so that you can control them. The very serious ones, such as serial bullying, have a massive effect and can overwhelm the recipient, as well as the person with the thoughts and behaviours.

Although we can articulate the shadow side, we are less willing to recognise these qualities in ourselves, even the benign ones. These facets include lying, gossiping and, more seriously, fraud, discrimination, and corruption. We can use these actions rarely or frequently.

If we utilise them, then it is likely we are stressed or in an adverse culture in which it is easier to default to the negative. If we use them all the time, then it can be that we like the negative effect we have, or we don't know what else to do.

We create 'stories' to justify our negative actions even when there is compelling evidence to the contrary.

> *It is only a small lie and won't hurt anyone.*

><

> *I don't care what she says; I did not bully her. My mother taught me to respect women.*

What guides us to choose the golden or shadow side will depend on our sense of Self and the balance we have between the two sets of qualities. Our past and current life guides our sense of Self. If we choose to have a positive and ethical sense of Self with care for others foremost, then we are likely to operate from the golden side. If we have a confident yet negative sense of Self, then we will work from the shadow side.

> *I do my best and most of the time. I am nice to most of the people in my team and guide them democratically in their work. The importance of self-care is something that I try to promote. I encourage my leaders to be positive and address any negativity that may occur.*

><

> *I tell the truth most of the time. Of course, lying or withholding information is a necessary part of work life. I do this and it does not affect my sense of Self, even when my manager spoke to me about*

*being honest. What is their problem? Can't they
see how much I achieve?*

❈

*And why shouldn't I take advantage of their poor
accounting systems? It's been working for me, and
I have tripled my income. It's their fault.*

REFLECTION

In the table below are some examples of golden and shadow
behaviours.

Golden	Shadow
Self-esteem, compassion, kindness, optimism, respect, decency, honesty, transparency, humility, well-being, integrity, diversity, communication, building relationships, collaboration, happiness, courage	Arrogance, manipulation, cruelty, insincerity, stubbornness, sneakiness, misusing banter deliberately, compassion fade/fatigue, hypocrisy, lying, dishonesty, laziness, malicious gossip, prejudice, discrimination, hubris, jealousy, envy, pessimism, competitiveness, revenge, psychopathy, sociopathy, Machiavellianism, narcissism, self-sabotage, underperformance, bullying, harassment, fraud, corruption, willful blindness, agnotology, suppression, plagiarism, fear, anger

Which golden and shadow behaviours do you use? How often? Ensure that this is an accurate picture of yourself. You can ask trusted people to verify your views. Then, complete the table below.

Frequency	Golden	Shadow
Daily		
Weekly		
Monthly		

CONSIDER

What is the effect of these behaviours on yourself and others? Positive, benign, or malignant?

What would others say about your behaviours?

Which ones protect you?

Which ones are hindrances?

What else could you connect to the golden and shadow, e.g., values, emotions, memories?

Which act as triggers?

Which ones maintain the golden or the shadow?

How do your work environment and colleagues affect your golden and shadow sides?

How harmonious is the balance between golden and shadow?

What reinforces and maintains the current balance between golden and shadow?

Where would you locate yourself on this continuum?

Golden and positive   Shadow and negative

←——————————————————————→

A FURTHER EXPLORATION OF GOLDEN AND SHADOW

Please select one or two of the practices below to help you explore, so that you can learn more about your golden and shadow aspects.

For about a week, make some time at the end of each day to reflect on which types of emotions, thoughts, and behaviours you have used, and why.

Who influenced you?

What was the purpose of your golden and shadow sides?

What was the balance between golden and shadow?

Which elements had protective qualities?

What role did your history have in your day-to-day life?

How much did you stop, pause, and consider the future?

Where would you locate yourself on this continuum?

Inclusive   Benign neglect of the positive   Malignant neglect of the positive

←――――――――――――――――――――――――――――→

Examples of being **inclusive** include listening and changing your mind when junior staff have a better idea; allowing freedoms in how work is done; letting people have control of their jobs; discussing any negativities openly and collectively so that there is a resolution; acknowledging that compromises are being made. Treating people decently.

Being clear about implementing purpose and values as much as possible is central to your being.

Benign neglect of the positive could mean that you manage the team but do not care about them; you just want to move on to the next step in your career. You aren't that interested in how work is done, just that staff achieve targets. The team must work around your needs and plans for holidays. The team is diverse, but you do not allow any adjustments unless a person pays for the changes themselves. You discuss purpose, but that is it; you don't take that discussion forward. Decency is just a word and an unnecessary one.

Malignant neglect of the positive could indicate that you are hostile toward the team. You shout and are not interested in anyone else's views. When staff make mistakes, you threaten them with pay cuts and negative appraisals. A close colleague has suggested a corrupt way of benefiting from your budget and you are considering it seriously. You have no interest in inclusion—people are there to work for you and their differences are their problem. The purpose is you, and values are the ones that benefit you.

Thinking about where you placed yourself on the spectrum…

Why have you adopted this stance?

How comfortable are you here?

What is your current approach to **courage and risk taking**? How positive is it?

From where did you learn your approach and what maintains it?

What alternative approach could you take?

What more could you do to develop yourself?

How open are you to **diversity, equity. and inclusion**?

What, within yourself, helps inclusion? What hinders it?

OTHER STERLING QUALITIES

The following are also very important qualities for you and your leadership. They include the factors outlined below that contribute to our overall leadership health. We are a blend of all of them. Let's investigate.

How compassionate and respectful are you with yourself and others?

What is the state of your physical health? And your mental health and overall well-being? What adjustments do you need to make daily because of your overall health?

Describe your known emotions and cognitions (how you think, listen, pay attention, decide, remember, and recall). How do you allow emotions into your work life? What or who provides you with energy and motivation?

How courageous are you at work? How much of a positive risk taker are you?

How hopeful and motivated are you?

What are your ethics, values, and sense of purpose? How much do you use them at work?

How important is it to be decent in all you say and do?

What have been your compromises? How do you live with the fact that you have compromised?

What is the impact of the different physical environments in which you function?

To what extent do you accept your own individual diversity? How inclusive are you of others?

How does your history influence you now?

MY RESPONSES

Please write your answers here.

THE PEOPLE IN
MY WORK LIFE

My outward Self and communication   Their outward Self and communication

My internal Self, shadow, biases, history   Their internal Self, shadow, biases, history

We each have an interconnected external and internal sense of Self from which we interact. It originates from our current and past life. Sometimes, we operate positively, and at other times, we communicate negatively.

There is a reciprocal relationship with people in our work lives. We influence each other's positives and negatives. Being with others who are supportive and caring can bring out those same qualities in us. The extent to which we are warm, inclusive, and democratic will massively influence the culture in which we lead.

Negativity can similarly affect ourselves, others, and the surrounding culture. It just takes one moment of awfulness to skew how people see us as leaders. If you shout once, people will remember, and then wait for it to happen again.

It is worth taking time to understand how others interact and communicate, and the extent to which they are positive and balanced, or negative.

REFLECTION

Using the space above, write all the names of key people in your work life.

Who is in your inner circle? Who is peripheral?

How decent is everyone to each other?

How do they influence you? What do you do when the influence is positive? What happens when it is negative?

How aware are you of your own interactive style? And what about the balance between your external persona and internal Self? What helps you stay positive? What takes you to the negative side? How do you regroup if you become negative?

> *I work well with Amanda, Joe and Isthanki. They are in my inner circle, and we understand and respect each other. They recognise when I am negative and let me know if I become 'shadow'. I can lie to get out of conflict and difficult situations. I am not as close to the rest, but that is fine. We*

all trust each other and know that, together, we get the job done.

❧

What a silly exercise. I don't understand the purpose of it. People are at work to achieve the mission of the organisation. I don't need to know anything else about them. I am fine with looking after myself and I know how to interact and communicate. That is enough.

Also, think about who is in your personal life and the impact those relationships have on you at work. Sometimes this happens, and it is best to know and acknowledge it.

INTERACTING WITH THE WIDER WORLD AND COMMUNITY

The arena in which we work has a subtle yet obvious impact on us. Physical space can be supportive or a deterrent to a positive approach. The resources we have make a tremendous difference. External and internal culture can help or hinder. Sustainability and climate change affect us and our organisations. Events in the country, region, and the world all have an impact. Think of how much the COVID pandemic affected us all.

It is important to understand the extent to which these factors affect us and the degree to which we can affect them. Please take some time to complete this table.

Issues	What is the impact (+ or -)?	What do I do to manage this issue?	Anything else?
At work–physical space, available resources, e.g., is there enough space?			
External and internal culture — e.g., what is the effect of culture on behaviour?			
Sustainability and climate change — e.g., do we pay enough attention to these factors?			
National, regional, and global factors (people and events) — e.g., how do global issues and leaders affect us?			

MY SENSE OF SELF AND COORDINATION

All the above qualities comprise your sense of Self and impact how you coordinate, and therefore function, in the world. You have now learned where you are on the continuum between golden and shadow.

Where would you like to be in five years' time? How would you like people to describe you and your leadership style? What image or sentence best describes the future you? Imagine stepping into the future you. How does it feel? Pretend you are looking back at the current you. Is the planned change enough? Or is less (or more) alteration needed?

> *I am learning about the balance between my golden and shadow sides. I sort of like and respect myself. But I want to get a better balance and see how I can address the shadow side when it occurs, as it always does when I am under pressure.*

I really don't understand why I must have extra coaching. My manager has said that I am too domineering. Nobody else has told me this before. She makes some sense. I suppose I could change a little. I don't want to.

What have you learned about yourself?

How coordinated and integrated is your current Self?

How would you describe your future Self?

WHAT HAVE YOU LEARNED?

Please use the table as a guide to summarise your reflections.

Area	Comments
Sense of Self and coordination Compassion, decency, and respect Well-being, mental health, and physical health Emotions, cognitions, physical (body), and relationships Hope, courage, risk taking, and motivation	

Influence of my history Current and future Self	
Presence and use of golden and shadow behaviours	
Values, ethics, and purpose	
People in my work life The people My interactive style	
Interacting with the wider world and community At work–physical space, available resources Where I live External and internal culture Sustainability and climate change National, regional, and global factors (people and events)	

Diversity, equity, and inclusion	

Based on your reflections and how you have completed the table, what have you learned about yourself? Please write a sentence or draw an image that describes you.

Who I am	

PLATINUM, GOLD, SILVER, OR BRONZE?

Now that you have carried out your personal assessment, what rating would you give yourself?

Platinum—an abundance of golden behaviours in many aspects of an individual or organisation; the golden is present and available 95% of the time or more. You address any minor shadow behaviours that arise, learn from them, and convert to the golden. All roles depict and use mostly golden behaviours. The need for decency is paramount.

Gold—continuous balance between golden and shadow behaviours for a leader or the organisation. The balance shifts and changes occasionally, but the golden is present at least 75% of the time. Shadow behaviours exist but are not significant enough to negate the impact of the golden. The shadow is being addressed slowly but surely. Roles depict and use golden behaviours. People try to be decent most times.

Silver–balance between golden and shadow, but the golden is variable and not present over 50% of the time. Daily events and circumstances influence the presence and use of golden or shadow behaviours. There are some efforts to promote the golden, but very few to deal with the shadow side. Roles focus on the use of shadow behaviours with a few golden behaviours. Decency matters only to some.

Bronze–preponderance of shadow behaviours. These are present 75% of the time or more, sometimes masquerading as golden behaviours. Acceptance and normalisation of shadow behaviours occur. There are token attempts to promote golden behaviours, but people recognise that these are not to be taken seriously. Instead, negative behaviours are tacitly and overtly rewarded. Roles encourage the use of shadow behaviours. There are very few attempts to be decent.

Note: The judgement of what 95% or 25% means is open and a personal qualitative decision.

The appendix contains more detail on each category.

My assessment is…

My reasoning for this assessment is…

Where would you like to be, overall?

GETTING READY TO CHANGE AND ACT

THE PATH OF CHANGE

The path of change

Readiness for change is an important factor. Going through the change process is much easier if you are already on the path to accepting the need for the change. You are more likely to let go emotionally of your existing life frame, keep what works and create new habits, and progress through closure and acceptance to your new life frame. It means that you are ready and willing to consider future options even though you cannot visualise them.

If a person is unaware or in denial of the need for change, even after a thorough analysis, then they are unlikely to go through the change process healthily. They may even resort to sabotage or just not take real action or force themselves to alter.

It is worth stopping to think about how you have changed in the past and map it onto the diagram so you can learn about how you are likely to change now. What was golden and shadow about how you altered?

Here are some key questions to consider:

Usually, how ready are you for change?

Ready, unaware, or resistant? How does this influence your path for change?

Current and future Self (think back to your earlier answers in this book)

Who is your current Self? Who would you like to be in the future?

Investigating the future

What can you do to imagine the future? What would help you think about the future and what it would look and feel like?

Emotions

What types of emotions have you shown and experienced when you have faced change? Which ones helped? Which ones hindered?

Sabotage

How could you sabotage your path to change? What preventative steps could you take to avoid doing this?

Emotional closure and acceptance

What or who could help you gain closure on your past Self?

Relapse

What could lead you to relapse to your old ways, e.g., becoming very stressed? What steps can you take to avoid relapse?

Changing habits (cognitively and practically)

What old habits and behaviours do you need to change? What could be your replacement habits and behaviours? How will you practise and ensure that you embed the new ones in your repertoire?

Hope, courage, risk-taking, and motivation

How much energy do you have for hope and courage for your journey? What or who will motivate you? How much of a risk-taker are you?

If you have used some shadow and toxic behaviours, how willing are you to let them go? What could help and what could hinder?

WHAT HAVE YOU LEARNED ABOUT YOUR APPROACH TO CHANGE?

How did you recognise the need to change? Which version of your Self was the starting point? What was the journey taken? What was the emergent and reshaped Self at the end of the journey?

I learned.......

Goodness, I thought I knew myself. It is amazing how we can build a story to protect our self-image. I thought I was the best leader compared to others. Being democratic and caring for people are positives for me. I need to investigate how I forget that when I am with other leaders who are arrogant and overconfident.

※※

Well, so what? I use a lot of negative and shadow behaviours to prevent change. It does not matter because the team is productive. Why should I change? They will have to make me.

BUILDING THE GOLDEN AND POSITIVE FOR OVERALL HEALTHINESS AND DECENCY

We have suggested some interventions for you to consider. We are using the concept of **overall healthiness**, incorporating living with the shadow side. All the elements interrelate and are codependent.

The key aspects of **overall healthiness** are:

> Sense of Self and coordination–compassion, respect, decency, well-being, mental health and physical health, emotions, cognitions, physical (body) and relationships, hope, courage, risk-taking, and motivation

Presence and use of golden and shadow behaviours
Values, ethics, and purpose
Interacting with the wider world and commu-
nity—material resources and the environment,
where the person lives and works
Diversity, equity, and inclusion
Administrative issues
History
Leadership and organisational interventions

We need most of these elements to become a healthier decent leader. However, we have a finite capacity for change. So, please choose what is vital and doable, and what will challenge and stretch you.

Pause for a few moments to honour history and its role in your present and future. What needs to be brought forward and what needs to be left behind? Please adapt our recommendations below so that they work for you.

A. SENSE OF SELF AND COORDINATION

The more integrated our sense of Self is, the easier it is for us to live, and to be in balance with our golden and shadow sides. It is worth understanding this and building up the core elements. Here are some suggestions.

Compassion, respect, and decency

It is important to have compassion for yourself and those you manage. Without true respect, compassion can lead to selfishness. You will be compassionate with anyone with whom you interact if you align your regard for the other person with compassion. This means that you shift from giving to make yourself feel better to sharing and supporting with dignity. Here are some interventions for you to try.

Building compassion

Make time to think about compassion in your life. You could start a contemplative practice if you have not already done so. Here are some possibilities.

> Create a time during your day to think about being compassionate. Write about the moments when you have shown compassion. How did others feel? Think about when others showed you compassion. How did you feel?

> Choose a picture or memory that depicts compassion for you. Sit and slow down your breathing. As it slows down, clear your mind, and dismiss any stray thoughts that appear. Now, in silence, focus on the picture or memory for five minutes. Then think about how this practice shifted your thinking, feelings, and body.

Consider a sentence that helps you think of being compassionate. Here is an example:

'We should, each of us, in all our choices, aim to produce the greatest happiness we can and especially the least misery.'

Richard Layard

Now write an essay to yourself about what this means to you in your life. Keep the essay and re-read it every week to remind yourself.

Openness to the future: What can you do to ensure that you remain compassionate, flexible, and open to the future? Perhaps you could allocate some time each day to pause, clear your mind, time, and heart, and just listen. What will you do to always honour this time?

Enhancing respect and decency

We can be pleasant without respecting the person we are being nice to; perhaps because they are not as qualified as we are. Why not stop and think about how much respect you have for the others in your life? How are the most-junior people treated? How do you show respect? What more could you do?

Compassion, respect, and decency in teams are best gained by activating the key elements of emotional intelligence.

Increasing interpersonal understanding involves making efforts to learn what work preferences team members have, and then incorporating them into work practices. How can you give people more control over their jobs?

Increasing awareness of team identity and group evaluation is another factor to be encouraged. How does the team function? How can they learn from mistakes without blame? What can they do to praise each other more?

Meaningful accountability, collective ownership, and responsibility also need to be encouraged so that people feel they are part of a greater mission.

It is now time to choose your actions and behaviours to bring into reality your intention for an improved Self with compassion, respect, and decency.

Based on the above, how would you describe your future sense of Self?

How can you create more compassion, respect, and decency in your life?

Which behaviours do you want to use to encourage greater compassion, respect, and decency in others? (For example, ask people to set aside 10 minutes at the start of the day to reflect on compassion, respect, and decency and how they will show it in their work, or make time to praise yourself and colleagues.)

1.

2.

3.

4.

What cues and triggers do you need to embed the behaviours? (For example, set an alarm that reminds you to be contemplative, or ask someone to check in with you about your progress.)

Remember, it takes 30 days for a new habit to embed itself in people's everyday behaviour repertoire and so you may need to be patient.

Well-being, mental health, and physical health

Well-being, mental health, and physical health have become very popular interventions in most sectors, especially during the COVID pandemic. Most well-being programmes will have a range of components: stress management, self-care, opportunities to learn about mindfulness, yoga, regular health checks, exercise, etc.

What do you do to maintain your well-being, mental health, and physical health? Having a good self-care plan that looks at physical health, well-being, mental health, finances and resources, and relationships will help. It is vital that you enact this, especially during stressful times when you are more likely to forget.

Emotions, cognitions, physical (body), and relationships

If a person's well-being, mental health, and physical health are in synchrony, then their emotions, cognitions, relationships, and bodies will also work for them, rather than against them. As individuals, we therefore have an extra obligation to do our utmost to look after ourselves. This includes those moments when we are not well or lack energy or motivation.

Hope, courage, risk-taking, and motivation

These are small but significant elements. They are present in us, but we may not always know or appreciate their strength and role in us changing. What or who could help you have more hope, courage, positive risk-taking, and motivation?

B. PRESENCE AND USE OF GOLDEN AND SHADOW BEHAVIOURS

Our shadow side is part of us and very unlikely to disappear. We must learn how to decrease its effect and learn to live more in the balance between the golden and the shadow side. Regular pause and reflection can help us do this. Here are some exercises to try.

Find a quiet and comfortable place (perhaps with a trusted person).

Write or draw your shadow side. Sit with your outputs and let the emotions arise. Wait until they have dissipated, then explore the purpose and function of these actions. Which parts of your golden side can help to counterbalance the shadow side? Then think about which shadow behaviours you can replace with a positive aspect, and which ones you could let go of.

On a second piece of paper, write or draw the replacement behaviours and emotions. Stop and let yourself feel. Then, when you are ready, say goodbye and destroy the first piece of paper or art. Keep the remaining paper or art.

This is an exercise you can repeat as often as you want.

Imagine talking to your shadow aspects and ask which ones need to stay or go. How can the golden side help with the shadow side? What has happened to the Self? Make a note of your reflections.

You could, on a daily or weekly basis, make some time to reflect on the extent to which you lived and worked from your golden side and/or the shadow side. What have you learned, and how will you cope from now on?

You could use the diagram below to reflect on your week. In which quadrant did you live and work? What have you learned and what needs to be improved or let go?

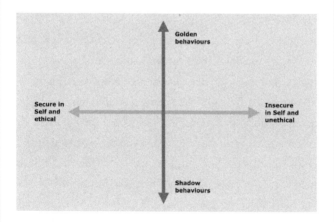

If you are someone who has dwelled on the shadow side and are ready to shift to using more golden aspects of yourself, then please start with celebrating the golden.

What is wonderful about you and your sense of Self?

Then note down your shadow parts and think about what you need to let go of to move to the golden side. Who and what will help you? What is the path you want to take?

❧

Sometimes, large changes are too much. You could start with small steps; for example, if ignoring people is one of your behaviours, you can make sure you greet colleagues. Some people may not believe the change at first, but if you persist, they are likely to adjust their perspective of you.

❧

Imagine a long line in a room from *Golden* at one end to *Shadow* at the other. Stand in the shadow part and look ahead to the golden part. Imagine that you are being accompanied by your best friend, *Decency*. Start walking towards the golden part and think about how you feel as you are moving towards it. Once you have arrived at the golden part, stop, and think about what/who could have helped you on your journey. What have you learned about yourself? What does your best friend, *Decency* 'say' to you? This could become a practice.

Based on her research in healing indigenous communities, Dr Sousan Abadian has created the Awareness, Responsibility, Imagination, Action (ARIA) framework, which can explore the shadow side. She intended it for healing individual and community trauma. The first step is to notice your Self and the erroneous assumptions, beliefs, and narratives.

Then consider your assumptions, beliefs, and narratives, and rewrite or replace them so that they are more positive and aspirational.

Third, become open to inspiration and the possibility of what the person or community wants to be, and focus on that instead of the current perspectives. Then use your aspirations to design next steps and act as though the desired future is here.

✺

Think about your life and how much balance there is between the golden and shadow sides. How would you describe this? How constant is the balance? What is the function and purpose of the balance for you? What could you do to ensure a healthier and more constant balance?

If you are working with and managing people who use shadow and toxic behaviours, what can you do?

First, make sure that you have solid evidence of their behaviours.

Then, it is only fair that you discuss their behaviours with them to help them acknowledge their actions and create a plan. It could help to give them the pocketbook we have produced for them to use, *Decency Journey: Your Own Toxic Work Behaviours.* If they still do not change, then you may need to consider their departure from the business.

You may have staff who have had to work in a toxic environment. They will need extra help and support. Please have a look at our pocketbook on this issue —*Decency Journey: Coping in a Toxic Environment.*

C. VALUES, ETHICS, AND PURPOSE

We have a sense of purpose and values for ourselves, and the organisation in which we work sometimes matches this. What we may ignore is the extent to which we compromise on purpose and values.

How much are your personal purpose and values central to your current work and life?

How are you coping with the inevitable compromise?

What else needs to happen for you to become comfortable with how you are living your purpose and using your values?

D. INTERACTING WITH THE WIDER WORLD AND COMMUNITY

Material resources and the environment

What we have and own in our life and work has a direct impact on us, as do our concerns about the lack of sustainability at the community and global levels.

Often, we have more than enough in terms of material goods. It is important to be aware of what is essential and necessary in your life and what is a luxury.

What more could you do to enable sustainability?

Where the person lives and works

Ensure that the physical environments in which you live, and work are sufficient. If they are not, how will you cope with the compromises and any associated stresses?

E. DIVERSITY, EQUITY, AND INCLUSION

Working towards inclusion is part of our job as leaders. It starts with our own perspective and experience of inclusion. What more could you do? Who can you bring into your life so that you continue learning about inclusion?

F. ADMINISTRATIVE ISSUES

There may well be some administrative issues that need to be addressed. For example, reviewing current HR policies to ensure that they promote golden, and not shadow, behaviours. If the latter is the case, then please make a note of them and work out a plan for change.

Another vital area is a trusted internal justice system such as a complaints procedure, investigation unit, and an ombudsperson.

You could think about introducing one or seeing what you need to make the existing system more operational and trusted.

G. HISTORY

Our individual history is very important and can still influence us daily. It is worth stopping and thinking about how your past has a daily impact. What do you need to keep and what do you need to let go of?

H. LEADERSHIP INTERVENTIONS

It is worth pausing and thinking about your leadership skills and style. How do you know that your current style is effective? How wide-ranging is your repertoire of leadership skills and behaviours? What more do you need to learn? There are many interventions you could choose. Please select one that not only helps you learn but also offers opportunities to practice and embed what you have learned. And which helps you look at both your golden and shadow sides.

PLANS FOR CHANGE

Here are some steps to take to devise your own plan for change. Use the questions to help you make notes in the table below.

Looking at the key areas for overall healthiness, which interventions will you select?

What will you do to live with the shadow side?

Think about your future Self? What type of leader do you want to be? And your promise, either to yourself, the organisation, or the wider world? What will be your role and likely impact?

What will be the key elements of your plan, and who will help you?

If you achieve all this, what overall rating would you give yourself in five years' time? Platinum, gold, silver, or bronze?

Area	Description	Time frame/ helpers
Sense of Self and coordination		
Compassion, respect, and decency		
Well-being, mental health, and physical health		
Emotions, cognitions, physical (body), and relationships		
Hope, courage, risk-taking, and motivation		
Presence and use of golden and shadow behaviours		
Values, ethics, and purpose		
Interacting with the wider world and community		

Material resources and environment		
Where the person lives and works		
Diversity, equity, and inclusion		
Administrative issues		
History		
Leadership and organisational interventions		
Anything else		

My overall rating will be:

A REALITY CHECK

Here is an opportunity for you to make sure that your plans are realistic and that you are ready. What changes do you need to make?

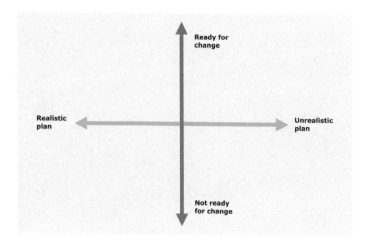

I am glad I took this journey to find a better balance between the golden and the shadow. I realise my wonderfulness and imperfections. This is going to be a long journey, but worth it.

Well, it made some sense. I am not sure I will follow up with the plan. My current approach works for me and the people I lead.

Thank you and we wish you the very best on your journey.
Please contact us if you have questions.
www.healthyleadership.world
Instagram: healthyleadership.world

REFERENCES

These are available on our website:
www.healthyleadership.world

APPENDIX

THE INDEX

Overall health level	Platinum	Gold	Silver	Bronze
Area/Elements				
Sense of Self and coordination	Very positive, stable, and connected in harmony with all elements (see below).	Positive, stable, and connected well to some elements (see below).	Sometimes positive and stable, rarely connected to other elements (see below), or not positively.	Not positive, maybe stable and disconnected or connected, but negative.
Compassion, respect, and decency	There is holistic compassion and respect for Self and all. Decency is very evident.	There is good enough compassion, respect, and decency at most times.	I give compassion and respect to those deemed to be worthy. I can be decent if I want to.	Very little compassion is available, and I give respect and treat people decently if I want to.
Well-being, mental health, and physical health	I take excellent care of Self and others.	I take good care of Self and others.	I take limited care of Self and others. Alternatively, I look after my Self and those deemed important.	I ignore personal health needs and those of others. Alternatively, I only look after my Self and those deemed important.
Hope, courage, risk-taking, and motivation	I am very hopeful and motivated. I am appropriately courageous and take good risks for the benefit of all.	I am hopeful and motivated. I am mostly brave and take good risks.	I am hopeful and motivated for selfish reasons. I am mostly either risk-averse or take foolish risks to benefit Self.	I am not hopeful or motivated by others. I avoid risks or only take risks if they are of benefit to Self and not the organisation.

Presence and use of golden and shadow behaviours	Golden>Shadow 95%	Golden>Shadow 75%	Golden=Shadow 50%	Golden<Shadow 25%
	I know and understand all my behaviours and focus very much on the golden side.	I know and understand most of my behaviours and focus mostly on the golden side.	I perhaps know and understand my behaviours and use mainly shadow behaviours.	I accept and only use shadow behaviours. My rationale can vary from being fine with their use to denying there is a problem.
External and internal culture, cognitions, emotions, physical (body), and relationships (including leadership)	External and internal culture and relationships are overall golden and positive.	External and internal culture and relationships are golden and positive.	External and internal culture and relationships are sometimes golden and positive.	External and internal culture and relationships are mainly shadow.
	Leaders (formal and informal) work together most of the time.	Leaders (formal and informal) work together sometimes.	Leaders (formal and informal) rarely work together.	Leaders (formal and informal) are always in conflict or work from the shadow side.
	I give compassion and complete respect to all.	I give compassion and respect to most.	I give compassion and respect to some.	I give compassion and respect to the favoured few.
	Work practices, styles of thinking, and decision-making are positive and helpful to the overall purpose.	Work practices, styles of thinking, and decision-making are sometimes positive and helpful to the overall purpose.	Work practices, styles of thinking, and decision-making are rarely positive and helpful to the overall purpose.	Work practices, styles of thinking, and decision-making enhance the shadow side and the express purpose of a few.
Values, ethics, and purpose	I actively use these as part of daily practice, in both thoughts and behaviours.	I use them on most occasions.	I use them sometimes.	I rarely use them.
	I am clear about my sense of purpose, which is shared and understood.	I am occasionally clear about my sense of purpose, which is sometimes shared and understood.	I am not clear about my sense of purpose, which is not shared. Alternatively, my sense of purpose is self-serving.	My sense of purpose is not positive and not shared or is completely self-serving.
Interacting with the wider world and community	I have meaningful interactions and incorporate sustainability fully.	I have useful interactions and incorporate sustainability most of the time.	I have spasmodic interactions and incorporate sustainability sometimes.	I ignore what is happening externally, or misuse it.

Material resources and the environment	There is sensible use of all resources.	There is mostly sensible use of resources.	There is a little sensible use of resources.	I use resources for personal gain.
Where the person lives and works	Very conducive to promoting the golden.	Helpful in promoting the golden.	Not very helpful in promoting the golden.	Not at all helpful, promotes negativity.
Diversity, equity, and inclusion	All are included and respected. Efforts are made to be inclusive.	Most are included and respected. Efforts are made to be inclusive.	There is lip-service to diversity, equity, and inclusion. Only the favoured are included.	Only those in the inner clique are included.
Administrative	I ensure that all administrative matters, e.g., policies, procedures, and strategies, reflect the golden side, and there are mechanisms to address the shadow side.	I ensure that most administrative matters, e.g., policies, procedures, and strategies, reflect the golden side and there are mechanisms to address the shadow side.	Few administrative matters, e.g., policies, procedures, and strategies, reflect the golden side, and there are hardly any mechanisms to address the shadow side.	I pay little attention to policies, procedures, and strategies, except for promotion and maintenance of the shadow side.
	I utilise fully these.	I ensure utilisation of most policies and procedures.	I utilise fully a few of these.	They are rarely used, or I misuse them to suit my purposes.
History	There is full acknowledgement of personal history, which is integrated with daily life.	There is general acknowledgement of personal history, which is integrated with daily life.	There is a brief acknowledgement of personal history, and I do not integrate it with daily life.	There is no acceptance of personal history. Denial is likely.
Leadership and organisational interventions	Every intervention that is introduced is helpful and useful. Staff are helped to implement what they have learned.	A traditional range of interventions is available, such as leadership programmes and coaching. Most staff benefit but there is less effort on helping them implement what they have learned.	Some interventions are available. Only a few have access and no effort is made to ensure that what is learned is applied.	There are a few interventions selected to benefit the few. No effort is made to ensure that staff apply what they have been taught.
Anything else?				

Printed in Great Britain
by Amazon

11967581R00047